The Seal of Melchizedek

Exploring the Modern Rebirth

of an Ancient Symbol

ALAN REX MITCHELL

ERNEST LEHENBAUER

The Seal of Melchizedek
Second Printing

IBSN 978-0-9842754-8-9

Greenjacket Books
Vernon, Utah

Table of Contents

About the Authors

Ernest Lehenbauer's father was an LDS convert from a long line of Lutheran ministers and an engineer for Ford Motor Company. His mother, a teacher, is of Mormon pioneer heritage. Ernest was therefore nurtured with a love of things both technical and spiritual, and was also blessed with an inquiring mind. When he heard a talk given by Bill Lewis, one of the designers of the San Diego Temple, it sparked his interest in the Seal of Melchizedek. Later Ernest traveled to the Middle East as an armored vehicle mechanic for a military contractor, where he began to notice the ubiquitous eight-pointed star. The ancient symbol continues to be of great interest to Ernest, who may be contacted at ernest@sealofmelchizedek.com

Alan Rex Mitchell wrote *Melchizedek's Seal & Scroll*, a treatise on all things Melchizedek and became acquainted with Ernest's zeal regarding the symbol, which ultimately led to this book. Alan has published in technical, scientific, economic fields, as well as fiction; his poetry was included in the latest Mormon poetry anthology, *Fire in the Pasture*. His novel, *Angel of the Danube*, was a critically acclaimed and is used in Mormon Literature classes. He may be contacted at: greenjacketbooks@gmail.com

Foreword

Alonzo Gaskill, author of *The Lost Language of Symbolism* and a religion professor at BYU, took an early look at the topic of this 8-point star symbol and observed that many people upon hearing the name "Seal of Melchizedek" assumed that the symbol was either directly associated with the ancient King Melchizedek of Genesis, or that it must be the symbol of the High Priesthood bearing his name. Gaskill concluded that the symbol points more to Christ than to either of the former two presumptions.

Independently we also came to similar conclusions. Perhaps you may also find that the symbol seems in so many settings to point heavenward, even towards Jesus Christ, so much so that it no longer seems random or mere coincidence. In any case, you can read, explore, and ponder for yourself. We hope you enjoy a personal journey of discovery, wherever it may lead you.

Ernest Lehenbauer
Alan Rex Mitchell

1

A Design for a Temple

On the short list of beautiful places in the world is La Jolla—Spanish for Jewel—California. Located 10 miles north of San Diego, the coastline is defined by a rugged hill that juts west, where it meets La Jolla Shores, the white sandy beach to the north. The San Diego Temple sits three miles inland just east of Interstate 5. The temple is a two-spire edifice unlike any of the hundred plus temples of the Church of Jesus Christ of Latter-day Saints. It was dedicated in 1993 after a lengthy and unique design period.

The LDS Church had originally bought property in San Diego, to the south, but when they found this plot available in La Jolla just off the interstate they jumped at the chance to purchase it. One of the desirable qualities of temple property is that it be close to traffic arteries and visible to the public. The injunction to not hide your light under a bushel applies equally to temples. But the La Jolla property brought challenges. The then-standard temple design followed the Boise, Idaho temple, which was a rectangle with 6 spires on the outer walls that was a nod to the Salt Lake Temple while remaining modern, simple, and straightforward. It would not fit into the La Jolla property either architecturally or aesthetically. The local architectural firm hired by the Church lobbied for the rejection of the "Boise" model and started over from the ground up. After listening to their appeal, the Church President Gordon B. Hinckley nixed an earlier directive to follow the Boise template, saying words to the effect that not all temples need to look alike.

With this new found freedom, the architectural firm went to work on a temple—taking their once-in-a-lifetime commission very seriously. The largely non-Mormon firm justified their enthusiasm by noting that the architect of Solomon's Temple, Hiram of Tyre, was not an Israelite at all. The questions they asked their LDS colleagues were fundamental and hearkened to the "form-follows-function" rule. What goes on in there? What are the traffic flows and times? In the back of their minds they asked: what can we build that would look like a temple and secure us a place in a pantheon of architect-gods?

William S. Lewis, Jr., a Latter-day Saint in the firm, wrestled with a basic design and motif. Bill Lewis fasted and prayed repeatedly, and either was inspired from a dream or woke up one morning with squares on his mind, depending on the version of the story. Although the preeminent 20th century architect Frank Lloyd Wright had decreed, "Destroy the box!" Lewis started with a box, or square, and began modifying it, tipping it, twisting it and tweaking it. He was much like a first-year architecture student brainstorming for an assignment to design a building using an

abstract shape. The firm settled on a floor plan with two boxes adjoining at the corners, like a blocky figure 8.

They applied their flow analysis and added more boxes at the junction to create rooms and hallways. They put boxes inside of boxes as the temple rose upward, and put square spires at the corners of boxes.

At the junction of the two taller boxes, or offset squares, they added a smaller box as an eight-sided atrium. Although the obligatory bronze angel Moroni stands atop the eastern spire, from an overhead perspective the center atrium is the critical location of the edifice. It is the point of tension holding the two primary squares together, like the gap between God's finger and Adam in the ceiling of the Sistine Chapel, and it is a circle surrounded by an 8-pointed star.

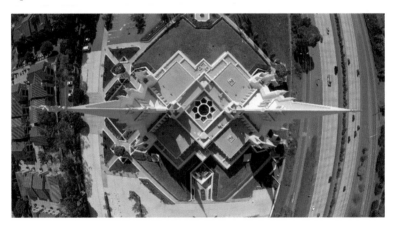

The circle typically represents perfection and eternity. The Mormon prophet Joseph Smith, in the King Follett Discourse, used the ring on his finger to explain how eternity has no end or beginning. The symbolist Michael S. Schneider observes that as a child, the "discovery and appreciation of the circle is our early glimpse into the wholeness, unity, and divine order of the universe."[1]

They built a model on a tabletop and tweaked it some more and then they took it on the road. The church leaders liked it. They kept using the squares as a motif in the detail work, taking the boxes and offsetting them by 45 degrees, using the offset squares in the

glass windows, inscribing them in the glass doors, and even using them in flower beds. They even put the offset square in the white wrought-iron fence that surrounds the grounds.

But what of the offset square that became the motif? Was it symbolic? The media touring the temple before the dedication posed this question to Elder David B. Haight.

"Probably just an architectural detail," he answered.

2

Identifying the Symbol

Stan Smith, a friend of architect William Lewis, had served as a Church representative during the temple project and took numerous pictures of the symbol. He decided it might be something more than just a detail.

Taking a trip to Salt Lake City, he visited the LDS Church Historians Office to inquire about the significance of the 8-pointed star. There he was referred to Hugh Nibley, noted Professor Emeritus of Ancient History at Brigham Young University. Nibley was legendary scholar of the ancient world and Mormonism, and a prolific author. When Stan Smith showed Nibley the symbol, he replied something to this effect: "Oh sure, it is the Seal of King Melchizedek."

Then Nibley showed Smith one of his latest books, *Temple and Cosmos* where, in the chapter *Sacred Vestments,* he had his illustrator Michael Lyon draw a reproduction of a mosaic from the Basilica of Sant' Appollinare Nuovo, a sixth century chapel in Ravenna, Italy. Although Nibley wanted to draw attention to the right-angled squares (or the Greek letter *gamma*) on the altar cloth, but Smith was more interested in the caption.

From Hugh Nibley, *Temple and Cosmos:*

> Another Ravenna mosaic, c. A.D. 520, shows the priest-king Melchizedek in a purple cloak, offering bread and wine at the altar (Genesis 14:18-20). The white altar cloth is decorated with two sets of *gammadia*, as well as the so-called "seal of Melchizedek," two interlocking squares in gold. Abel offers his lamb as Abraham gently pushes Isaac forward. The hand of God reaches down to this sacred meeting through the red veils adorned with golden *gammadia* on either side. The theme is the great sacrifice of Christ, which brings together the righteous prophets from the past as well as the four corners of the present world, thereby uniting all time and space. [2]

As seen in the photograph above, on the altar cloth are two sets of four Greek alphabet gamma (Γ), plural *gammadia*, also called the Masonic or carpenter squares. Nibley was emphasizing these *gammadia* in his chapter on sacred vestments. In addition to these figures on the altar cloth, the design is also found on the curtains at either side, forming a box that defines a holy place; and there between them is found the symbol of two overlaid squares…the 8-pointed star.

Stan Smith had discover the connection to the inspired design to the San Diego Temple!

Nibley is not the only scholar to link the symbol with Melchizedek. Constantin Marin, in a Byzantine journal, connected Melchizedek with the star from the mosaics altar cloth shown at the Basilica of San Vitale, also in Ravenna, Italy, which contains depictions of "Christian" sacrifices of the Old Testament that were types of the Sacrifice of Christ. This mosaic shows Abel offering a lamb at the altar as a type of the Lamb of God or the Messiah to come; Melchizedek is at the other side of the altar offering up the holy meal of bread and wine (Genesis 14:18-20).

According to Constantin Marin:

> The star on the table cloth of the altar table of the representation
> 'Melchizedek's Sacrifice' [see above] receives, in the context of Holy
> Text, the power of a symbol expressing the Divine Essence of
> Melchizedek. [3]

To repeat, Marin viewed the star as symbolizing "the Divine Essence of Melchizedek." One could interpret this as "The qualities of God", or the Priesthood. It is not strange to think the Seal of Melchizedek represents the Holy Priesthood.

A third mosaic, that of Empress Theodora (below) in the Basilica of San Vitale, exhibits the Seal of Melchizedek on the tunic of her first attendant, and variations on others. Note the brown squares on the tunics of the clergy to her left, possibly signifying priesthood. Further, note the imagery of the pulled-back curtain as in the first Melchizedek mosaic, only this time it is decorated with 4-pointed symbols. Observe that Theodora's first attendant is wearing and demonstrating the Seal of Melchizedek—perhaps to signify her devotion or a holy order.

Smith reported his findings to Bill Lewis, who was compelled to take the trek to Utah and visit with Nibley himself to have it confirmed. Since Nibley typically spoke quickly and assumed everybody knew as much as he did, it may have been difficult for Lewis or Smith to follow the complete conversation and later report all the connections of the symbol. Because President Hinckley had taken such an interest in the temple design, Lewis wrote him a letter reporting the discovery.

After retiring, Bill Lewis served as a worker in the temple he designed. He has spoken at over a hundred gatherings about his experience as a temple architect. Although the symbol is now quite familiar to Church members in the San Diego area, it is generally unknown to Church members at large.

Bloggers have been instrumental in finding and conveying information on the symbol. LDS blogger Bryce Haymond at *Templestudy.com* had also heard stories from San Diego about the symbol in 2008, and contacted Bill Lewis who related his story.[4] Haymond noted that since the dedication of the San Diego Temple, the Seal of Melchizedek symbol has been used for the chandelier of the Newport Beach, California Temple, and the new glass doors to the entrance of Salt Lake Temple with a beehive in the center (as shown below.)

Another blogger, Tim Barker at *ldsstudies* found the comments by Marin mentioned earlier, as well as connections to the Seal found in other cultures, in the number 8, and with the prophet-king Melchizedek himself. More on these later.

Co-author Ernest Lehenbauer was also instrumental in hunting down the symbol. His story in his own words:

I was living in the beautiful San Diego area. Not only had I become a loyal fan of the beautiful weather in southern California, but the stunning San Diego Temple quickly became my favorite place of worship. Coming from a long line of Lutheran ministers on my Father's side, and a solid pioneer ancestry of Latter-day Saints on my mother's side, I pondered deeply the principles of the gospel and the mysteries of temples and symbolism.

One Sunday night I chose to attend a Fireside talk given by one of the three head architects of the San Diego Temple architectural firm. As the topic of the 8-point star symbol that influenced the temple design was presented, I was particularly enthralled.

I was even more intrigued when I heard the name as presented by Hugh Nibley: The Seal of Melchizedek. I pondered the power of a symbol upon which not only an entire temple was designed, but one that also bore such a significant name.

I heard directly from one of the architect team partners that designed the San Diego Temple, who explained that the designer saw this symbol in a dream and based the floor plan and décor of the temple on this design; namely two offset, intersecting squares. Much like the 6-point Star of David but with 8 points instead.

Then life happened and time passed. I began traveling and working in the Middle East as a sub-contractor for the Department of Defense. I soon started a blog to share my adventures with friends and family.

I first noticed the so-called "Seal of Melchizedek" when a fellow LDS soldier and friend showed me some pictures. There it was on a bridge in Kirkuk, Iraq, where I was working on an air base. Soon thereafter I began noticing the shape of the star in almost every Mosque tower. As I traveled in Middle East countries such as Afghanistan and Kuwait, and also throughout Europe, I began noticing it in many places. I decided it was time to get serious and do more research. I suspected the symbol would be found in many cultures, possibly because it had a common source anciently. If true, then similar examples might be found throughout history as well.

Ernest began searching the scriptures for references to the number 8 and found it associated with rebirth. He found the 7 days of the creation meant, in the Hebrew tradition, whole or complete. (Gen. 2: 1-2) while the 8th day becomes the first day of a new period or a beginning.

In the Law of Moses, a sacrificial lamb (or ox) was to be kept with its mother until the 8th day (Exodus 22:30). Similarly, male Hebrew children were also kept at home 7 days, but on the 8th day, they were taken to the tabernacle or temple to be circumcised and consecrated to the Lord (Gen 17:12; Luke1:59). John the Baptist and Jesus were both subjected to this ritual as infants.

The priests of Levi that officiated at the Tabernacle were to complete 7 days of purification, and on the 8th day were permitted to enter the temple (Leviticus 8:35, 9:1). This purification was mentioned centuries later by the prophet Ezekiel: "...*upon the eighth day, and so forward, the priests shall make your burnt offerings upon the altar and your peace offerings; and I will accept you, saith the Lord*" (Ezekiel 43:26-27). Solemn assemblies were held on the 8th day after a feast (Lev. 23:36; Neh. 8:18).

In the rebirth of civilization, or the great flood, there were eight souls were saved on Noah's Ark (1 Peter 3:20), and the earth was "baptized" to cleanse a filthy world—another example of a new, pure beginning, and a symbolic reflection of the ordinance of baptism (Genesis 8:16).

At the end of his earthly ministry, the resurrected Christ appeared to the apostles following his atonement and crucifixion "after eight days" (John 20:26). It is no coincidence that the Lord changed the Sabbath from the 7th day to the 8th day, or the first day of a new week, and instituted the sacrament on that day (Acts 20:7). Today, the Latter-day Saints celebrate a new beginning each week by partaking of the sacrament and remembering the atonement of Christ (D&C 59:9).

As told in the Book of Mormon, the inaugural prophet Lehi and his family wandered 8 years in the wilderness, leaving an old corrupt homeland and sailed over the ocean (symbolic of baptism); finally arriving in a new promised land (1 Ne 17:4).

Similarly, centuries before Lehi, Jared and his brother took their families, left the corrupt Babel and sailed forth in 8 vessels to a new, pure beginning. This time, their vessels were literally buried in the water as they crossed the ocean.

Baptism, as a type of the death and resurrection of Christ, is also associated with the number 8; in the Doctrine and Covenants (68:27), the proper age for children to be baptized is declared to be at age eight.

Ernest found the scriptures referring to the number 8 to be concerned with purification, sacrifice, and beginning a new life.

3

The Symbol in History

The 8-pointed star is found through history and across many cultures—usually in relation to deity. In ancient Babylonia, an 8-pointed star represented the planet Venus and was associated with the mother-goddess Ishtar, or Inanna, although it sometimes designated the King of Babylon.[5]

Similarly, ancient religion of the Balts—ancestors of the Latvian and Lithuanian people—used an 8-pointed star *Ausekla Zvaigzne* that represented the Morning Star (Venus) and was a symbol for the goddess *Ausrine*, daughter of the sun—the personification of the planet Venus. Representing their highest god, the 8-pointed star with a circle was the goddess of fertility, another symbol of renewal, or a new pure beginning.

Excavation of the royal tombs of ancient Ur found several 8-pointed flowers on royal headdress (below); and the star-flowers (on the right) depicting a ram feasting on a tree. It is likely the Venus star in both represented royalty and possibly the tree of life.[6]

The distinctive shape of the Seal, expressed as a flower or leaf in the days of Abraham and Melchizedek, is found centuries and millennia later. In every case, the symbol is associated with deity, sacred writings, or leadership.

Star of Lakshmi

Hinduism has eight pointed stars dating to antiquity, and the double offset square is the Star of Lakshmi, an important Hindu goddess. Lakshmi presides over *eight* sources of wealth: godly identity, grain, courage, animals, progeny, victory, knowledge, and money.

Early Christianity

Third Century Coptic Christian Burial Cloth

What we call the Coptic Church is the Egyptian form of Christianity; the Coptic Church claims a direct evolution beginning with the visit of the Holy Family to Egypt when Jesus was a young boy. Historically it was Saint Mark the Evangelist, during the first century AD, who is considered to be the founder of the church.

In 1920, English archeologist Albert Kendrick reported on textiles from Egyptian graves dating from 2nd to 4th century A.D. excavated at Akhmim, Egypt had several textiles with the double-offset square and others with the circle inside.[7] Kendrick was astute enough to note that the symbol found in later mosaics in Ravenna and Byzantine art may have had Egyptian roots, and that these symbols endured as Christian symbols from the 2nd to the 5th

Textiles from Egyptian Graves, Kendrick (1920)

century. The Coptic textiles show that the 8-pointed star was a symbol of Christ for centuries prior to the crucifix symbol.

Later, the Christian altar cloths evolved so that the Seal was replaced with a cross, whose watershed moment came when Constantine marked a cross on battle shield. The cross in the form of a crucifix did not appear until the 5th century, although the cross had been a symbol in early Christianity.

Prior to Christ, the Egyptian *ankh* cross was a symbol of life. The *Tau* cross was also symbol of righteousness centuries before the Christian era. In Ezekiel 9:1-6 the prophet is commanded to place a mark on those who mourn the wickedness of the city Jerusalem, where "mark" is literally translated *Tau*. (See also Alma 39:9 where Alma advises his son Corianton to cross himself relative to temptations.)

Christians in 5th Century

Other Christian art and architecture from the 5th century was constructed with octagonal design. Many structures are octagonal in shape, including the Church of Nativity in Bethlehem, and St. Peter's house in Capernaum (below).

The number 8 is traditionally associated with the concepts of rebirth, renewal, resurrection, and baptism. Eight also represents movement to a higher spiritual level. Early baptismal fonts were octagonal, and occasionally the entire structure was 8-sided; for example, the Basilica of San Vitale in Ravenna, Italy.

The Martyrium of Saint Philip in Hierapolis (Holy City), near Pamukkale, Turkey was part of an early Christian pilgrimage complex that was abandoned in the 14th century. The Martyrium housing the grave of St. Philip was constructed in the 5th century but only uncovered in the last few decades. Note the doorway arch above whose keystone displays the Seal of Melchizedek (insert).

5th Century Baptism Font, Milan, Italy

As mentioned earlier, during the 5th century baptism fonts were characteristically constructed in octagonal shape, signifying the resurrection as shown above in ruins from Milan, Italy (previous page).

Baptistery in St. Joseph Cathedral, Missouri

Even though the mode of baptism has been changed by much of Christianity, the shape of fonts has carried over until day. In the Baptistery above, the octagonal font is surrounded by the purple tile Seal of Melchizedek. The baptistery below has the symbol of water, as well as a circle in the center. Like many baptisteries, it has separate entrances and exits to denote the path to a new life.

St. Paul the Apostle Catholic Church in Westerville, Ohio

Blogger "Hamblin of Jerusalem" recognized this Seal of Melchizedek from an ancient Christian church near Khirbet Beit Sila, Israel. The Byzantine era mosaic has since been moved to the museum *Inn of the Good Samaritan*, according to William Hamblin, Professor of History at Brigham Young University.

Where ever Christianity went, themes of baptism, holiness, eternity, and resurrection followed. The Seal of Melchizedek can be found even in places as far off as Russia. This Russian Orthodox icon of the Virgin with Holy Child is framed by the circle at the center, and two overlain stylized squares. Also present are the symbolic images of angels, lambs, and lions.

Jewish Culture

The Leningrad Codex has the "carpet page" or *cover* that shows a 6-pointed star (*magen David*) inside an octagon, which in turn is inside an 8-pointed star inside a circle inside a square. The Codex is the oldest known Jewish scripture dated 1008 AD.

It is interesting that the *Magen David*, or the six-point Star of David, was only adopted on the national flag of the state of Israel in 1948. It became a symbol for Jewish Zionism only a few decades before that, making it a relatively modern choice. But both the 8-point and 6-point stars are still familiar and common to culture in Jerusalem.

Islamic Symbol

With the ascent of Islam, the 8-pointed star was adopted by the growing conquest throughout the region. Known in Arabic as *Rub el Hizb*, its meaning can vary in translation. Literally, *Rub* is quarter and *Hizb* is group, thus "quarter group" because it marked the quarter points in the Koran, where the symbol was inserted—

a practice not uncommon among Arabic printers today. Another less-used translation puts *Rub* as "leader," as in "leader of the group," or "leader of the people."

Clever versions of symbol are still popular throughout the Islamic world among businesses and government entities, such as this one for the Kuwait Stock Exchange.

A mosque in Kuwait (below) exhibits the symbol on and around the dome, as well as the octagonal shape of the call tower.

A more interesting name for the *Rub al Hizb* is the Arabic *Khatim sulaymon*, or **"the seal of the prophets,"** according to a Moroccan design expert.[8] *Seal* in this context, refers to an imprint made by a signet ring in wax—and ancient and medieval practice to verify the authorship and authority of the sender. Extending the definition—the "seal of the Prophets" could be rendered "the authority of God's messengers."

The Breath of the Compassionate

When Moslem designers placed the *Rub al Hizb* next to each other the void between them creating a pointed cross. Note the black voids interspaced with the *Rub al Hizb* above to form *The Breath of the Compassionate* in Islamic tradition. According to Schneider,[9] the design is a cosmological model symbolizing the interplay of polar opposites through which the creation ensued. To clarify symbolically, the base square represents the four elements of the earth (earth, fire, air, water) and the offset diamond represents the four qualities of dry, wet, hot, cold—and the creation results from their interplay. Because "the Compassionate" is the 99th name of Allah in Islamic tradition, the name suggests the Creator spoke and the world came in being—in other words, the Compassionate breathed.

The *Rub el Hizb* is found in oriental rugs from the Middle East ever since they were considered fashionable during the middle Ages. Many of the decorative rugs were featured in medieval paintings where the *Rub el Hizb* was included. For example, this portrait of portrait of King Henry VIII standing on a carpet with a *Rub al Hizb* design.[10]

To this day, two interlocking squares with an interior circle mark a prominent space in the decorative floor in the House of Lords, England.

Masonic Symbol

Another connection with Melchizedek was linked to the Latter-day Saints' nineteenth-century mentors in symbolism, the Free Masons. Joseph and Hyrum Smith were Master Free Masons at the time of their martyrdom, and the predominant Masonic symbols of the compass and the square likewise have a significant place in LDS temple worship.

One off-shoot of the Free Masons in England used the double offset square in the center of their rendition of the Egyptian god, *Kneph*, to form the masthead of their journal named *The Kneph*. The Egyptian deity *Kneph* (soul breath) represented the life-force whose breath brought gods and man into existence. The Masons used the image of a winged egg to show the potentiality of man with wings of heaven; in other words, the breath of life that has unlimited potential. The all-seeing eye is at the center of the double-offset square; in other words, the seal of the all-seeing God.

Later Egyptian Christians transformed *Kneph* into what symbolist Howey called "the Christos of the Gnotics."[11] The first century Egyptian Christians had simply integrated "the breath of life" into their new religion.

Henry Pelham Holmes Bromwell, an nineteenth-century English Mason, published a Masonic symbol book with an eight-pointed star called *the Signet of Melchizedek*—the 47th Problem of Euclid.[12]

It was made by taking a line and drawing a second line of equal length at a 45 degree angle, and then repeating until you arrive back at the original point. It takes a total of eight lines to circumnavigate 360 degrees.

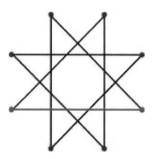

Bromwell writes:

> **The Signet of Melchisedek**, King of Righteousness and Priest of the Most High God; King of Schalaam, which is King of Peace—the Octalpha or eight-fold endless triangle, which, being a geometric figure composed of lines continually [13]reproduced to infinity, by Right Angles, Horizontals, Perpendiculars and Diagonals, was hailed by our Ancient Brethren among all nations, **as the Symbol of the Divine Omnipotence, Omniscience and Omnipresence**; universal, infinite and eternal.

A signet is a finger ring used to certify authority by impressing a wax seal on an official document. According to Bromwell, the Signet of Melchizedek is a symbol of the Divine.

The reader may note that the above 8-pointed star is not the same as the Seal of Melchizedek with its overlapping squares. In fact, the signet star is frequently seen in patterns of American quilts where it is known by several names: the simple star, Ohio Star, Maryland Star, Texas Star, Lone Star, Polaris, and Bethlehem star.

Eight in Architecture

The European tradition of including the symbol as a star or octagon in religious structures was carried over into the Americas at the time of the settling of the new world. Here you can see the 8-point star windows in this Catholic structure in Quito, Ecuador. The windows in churches were often 8-sided or pointed to symbolize Christ: As light comes through the windows, so the source of light is Christ, or comes from Him. Note the interior circle as a symbol of eternity that often accompanies the 8-point star.

Like the 8-sided star, octagonal steeples evolved in Europe and were carried over into New World architecture. Usually they were built on a square base, then continued upward into a spire. The <u>square base</u> of the tower can symbolize the earth in its four quarters, or four seasons, etc. Next comes the 8-sided belfry with an optional 8-sided lantern on top; both are symbolic of Christ, or rebirth through the atonement. At the apex is the spire pointed to heaven. The entire steeple symbolism denotes that the way to get from earth to heaven is through renewal in Christ.

Steeples of Mormon temples from early days of the church used this typical octagonal form. The St. George, Utah temple, dedicated in 1877, followed the same design using the square base, the octagonal belfry and lantern, and the spire rising above.

St. George Temple

4

Modern Rebirth

Over the centuries, the symbolism associated with the octagonal shapes in Christian architecture and art appears to have diminished. With the advent of the San Diego Temple, we find it more in temples and also in some stake centers, such as the one in American Fork, Utah pictured below. It has the traditional 8-sided steeple, as well as 8-part windows over the doorway that implies that one enters through Christ.

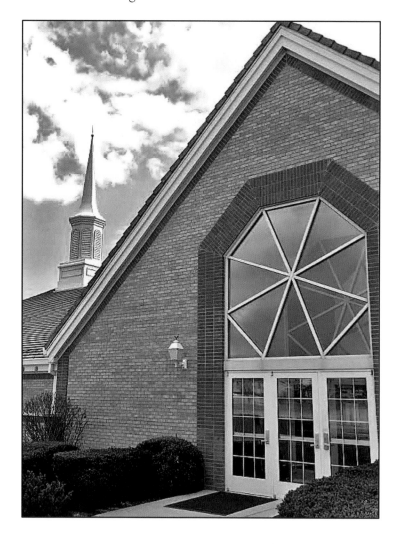

The Seal of Melchizedek has begun appearing in more temples, perhaps most significantly being added to the new entrance of the Salt Lake City temple. Although the familiar shape can be found in chandeliers, carpets, and other interior decor, it is also often found at the entrance, as in the glass doors pictured below, where the beehive symbol of Deseret, is placed in the center of the star.

The Seal of Melchizedek is found at the entrance of the New Mexico Temple (left) in a threefold expanding design, which might be symbolic of the Godhead; or alternately, of their eternal power that expands through the three realms of past, present, and future as we gain salvation through them.

The **Conference Center at Temple Square** was built after the San Diego Temple. The Seal of Melchizedek be added to the new Salt Lake Temple entrance and lobby at about the same time. It shouldn't be surprising then that 8-point stars also occur throughout the structure, design, and décor of the new Conference Center at Temple Square, as shown below.

5

Latter-day Meanings

Stars were symbols for deity in ancient religions. We have seen the 8-pointed flower/star headdress found in the tombs of ancient Ur, and the Venus goddess in ancient Babylon. The number 8 has also been associated with right living in the Egyptian 8 roads, the Buddhist 8 paths, and the Hindu 8 forms of wealth.

Likewise, stars are symbols of Christ and angels in religious tradition; such as in the book of Revelation where Christ is described as the "bright star of dawn" (Rev. 22:16), and in Matthew 2:2-9 and 3 Nephi 1:21 where a new star was the sign of Christ's birth. Writing to the early saints, the apostle Peter spoke of the star as a symbol of Christ:

> We have also a more sure word of prophecy; whereunto ye do well that ye take heed, as unto a light that shineth in a dark place, until the day dawn, and the day star arise in your hearts. (2Peter 1:19)

The star was the central motif of Val Brinkerhoff's two volume photographic exposé, *Day Star*.[14] Brinkerhoff is professor of visual arts at Brigham Young University who has photographed religious symbols in architecture 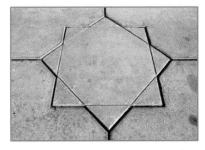 throughout the world. In *Day Star;* he continually emphasizes that the various styles of the star are symbols of life, and through this association they represent the Savior of mankind.

Alonzo Gaskill, a BYU professor of religion specializing in symbolism, opines that the Seal of Melchizedek ought **not** to be associated with the prophet-king contemporary with Abraham; rather it is representative of rebirth and resurrection and it is "a symbol for the atoning sacrifice of the Lord Jesus Christ."[15] He demonstrates how the number 8 and the 8-pointed star is symbolic of renewal, rebirth, and resurrection and is linked to the Savior.

Symbolic Interpretation

According to the mystical tradition of Islam called Sufism, the earth's symbol is the box square, the diamond represents the cardinal points or directions—in this they agree with symbol interpretation worldwide.

Earth   cardinal points, light   heaven

An encyclopedia on symbolism defines the two offset squares, or the eight-pointed star, as: *"Material generation through the interaction of two opposing principles."*[16] These opposing principles represented by the box and the diamond are, in this case, the world and the light. The box/diamond could also represent dualities such as man/woman, or matter/spirit.

Sufism holds that the crossing of these squares was used by the Egyptians to symbolize the 8 roads to heaven.[17] Similarly, Buddhism has its eightfold path; and Christianity its 8 Beatitudes. All describing righteousness, which in ancient Hebrew (*tsedeq*) was connected to prosperity—just as Hindu's Lakshmi's star represented the 8 forms of wealth. Interestingly, the goddess' wealth are 4 parts earthly (grain, animals, victory, money) and 4 parts spiritual (knowledge, progeny, courage, godly identity). Which brings us back to the square earth and the diamond of light contain in the Seal.

Just as early Christians used the octagon to represent rebirth, the octagonal Seal of Melchizedek easily symbolizes the **Resurrection and Rebirth.** The square would represent the earth and mortality in that Jesus was made flesh. The diamond would represent the Light of the World (John 8:12) and the new body that Jesus took up and which also awaits us (Philippians 3:21).

Eternal Marriage, or the new and everlasting covenant of marriage, can be symbolized as the raising of the earthly square to a spiritual square and sealed by God. Alternately, the first square can represent the man and the second square the woman, because in many cultures the diamond shape symbolizes feminine life-giving powers. When the squares are interwoven they may symbolize man and woman linked together in each of four aspects of life, i.e., physical, intellectual, emotional, and spiritual. The circle then represents the eternal power to bind on earth what is bound in heaven (Matt. 16:19). It is no wonder the Seal has become part of the architecture in our temples.

The offset squares are symbols that live through the ages, finding its way into unexpected corners of our lives. The **Talmadge Family Cross Stitch** contains all the elements of the Seal of Melchizedek with some variation. First the box, then the diamond within, and the circle inside the diamond. Note the red 8-petalled rosettes at the 4 points of the circle, and the hearts at the points. Inside the circle at the center is the family name.

This diamond-inside-box symbol is called the *goddess weave*[18] and can, like the seal, be found in the Ravenna mosaics on the tunics of the queen's attendants (see page 8).

Symbol of the King of Righteousness

Melchizedek (*melchi tsedeq* in Hebrew) translates as King of Righteousness although there is considerable wordplay as the King of Salem (see Heb. 7:2; Alma 13:17, JST Gen. 17:33). The word *tsedeq* originated from an earlier Canaanite word and can be translated as righteousness, justice, prosperity, and peace. In  ancient times, there was a linguistic connection between *peace* and moral living, prosperity, and a non-stressful life. Righteous living is associated with the number 8, and the prominence of the Seal on the altar cloth of Ravenna is not out of place. The title, *melchi tsedeq*, or King of Righteousness, can be also translated as Prince of Peace (JST Gen. 17:33), another name for Christ. In other words, the name Melchizedek may represent "*The Righteous*," as Enoch called him (Moses 7:45.47) and as John named him (1John 2:1); or "*Righteous Judge*," as Paul referred to him (2Tim 4:8). The 20th century stained glass rendition of Melchizedek (left) shows him with facial features similar to depictions of Jesus.

In his book *Melchizedek's Seal & Scroll* (2012), Alan Rex Mitchell shows that an early 4th century Christian scripture from Nag Hammadi, Egypt included a book *Melchizedek* that frequently uses the name of Melchizedek to represent Jesus Christ.[19] Mitchell also analyzes the Dead Sea Scroll *Melchizedek* (11Q13) that describes a messianic figure who will come to Jerusalem at the meridian of time to fulfill prophecy, make atonement for the sons of light, exact judgment on Belial, and transfer his dominion to the saints of Zion.

Using Melchizedek—*King of Righteousness*—as a name for Christ goes hand-in-hand with the Lord's revelation on the priesthood (D&C 107:1-4) in which we are told that the ancient church used the name Melchizedek for "*the Holy Priesthood after the Order of the Son of God*" to avoid frequent repetition of his name. The Seal of Melchizedek symbol becomes, in its truest sense, the signet of Christ—the Righteous King.

Images

Images contained in this book that are not attributed below are © 2015 by Ernest Lehenbauer; otherwise:

p. 4. San Diego Temple Video photo capture by Brandon Brigham, <https://www.youtube.com/watch?v=trB8aLerqDo> Oct 22, 2014

p. 6. Ravenna mosaic. Basilica of Sant'Apollinare in Classe

p. 7 The Offerings of Abel and Melchizedek (detail of the hand of God), 526-548AD, mosaic. Basilica of San Vitale, Ravenna, Italy

p. 8 Mosaic of Empress Theodora. Basilica of San Vitale, Ravenna, Italy

p. 13 Venus star. Headdress. "Ram in Thicket." Last two images from ancient Ur found at sumerianshakespeare.com

p. 14 Plate 3 from Kendrick (see note 8 below) p. 146.

p. 15 Plate 4 from Kendrick, (see note 8 below.) p. 164.

p. 16 Remains of Byzantine Church. *Biblical Archeology Review* (Sep/Oct 1993)

p. 17 Martyrium of St. Philip at Hierapolis; Baptism Font, Milan, Italy

p. 18 Baptistery in St. Joseph Catholic Church courtesy of Inside/Out Architecture, Inc., Ballwin, MO, insideoutarch.com; Baptistery in St. Paul the Apostle Catholic church in Westerville, Ohio

p. 19 Christian Mosaic from Khirbet Beit Sila, photo courtesy website "Hamblin of Jerusalem: Seal of Melchizedek", used by permission. Russian icon at http://www.azerbaijanrugs.com.

p. 19 Leningrad Codex carpet page.

p. 23. Portrait of King Henry VIII. Belvoir Castle. Unknown artist. 17th century after Holbein. at http://www.azerbaijanrugs.com

p. 24 The Kneph masthead.

p. 31 Photo by Ernest Lehenbauer, sidewalk "Bethlehem star" Quito, Ecuador

p. 33 Talmadge family cross stich photo by Rochelle Talmadge; used with permission.

p. 34 Melchizedek stained glass from St. Timothy Catholic Church, Los Angeles, CA

p. 36 Front cover, *Melchizedek's Seal & Scroll*, Greenjacket Books, Vernon, Utah

Notes

1 Michael S. Schneider. *A Beginner's Guide to Constructing the Universe*: Mathematical Archetypes of Nature, Art, and Science. Harper Perennial (1995)

2 Hugh Nibley. *Temple and Cosmos; beyond this ignorant present*. (1992.) The collected works of Hugh Nibley Vol. 12 Ancient History. Deseret Book Co. and FARMS. p. 109.

3 Constantin Marinescu Marin, *Jahrbuch der Österreichischen Byzantinistik* [Yearbook of Austrian Byzantine Studies] 32/6 (1982) 317.

4 Bryce Haymond. Templestudy.com

5 Tim Barker. *Seal of Melchizedek Eight-pointed Star*. Found at http://lds-studies.blogspot.com/2011/05/seal-of-melchizedek-eight-pointed-star.html
6 Ur images found at sumerianshakespeare.com
7 Albert F. Kendrick. Majesty's Stationary Office, London, England, (1920) *Catalogue of Textiles from Burying-Grounds in Egypt*, 1: Vol. 1 Graeco-Roman Period. Found at http://books.google.com/books?id=92m1AAAAIAAJ Book is in possession of the author and past copyright.
8 moroccandesign.com/eight-point-star.
9 Schneider, op cite. p. 274.
10 King Henry VIII. Belvoir Castle. Unknown artist. 17th century after Holbein. at http://www.azerbaijanrugs.com/mp/unknown_henryVIII_belvoir.htm
11 M. Oldfield Howey. *The Encircled Serpent: A Study of Serpent Symbolism in All countries and Ages*. (1955). Noble Printers, Inc., New York, NY
12 Tim Barker. "The Seal of Melchizedek" in LDS Studies (August 8, 2010) http://lds-studies.blogspot.com/2010/08/
13 Henry Pelham Holmes Bromwell, *Restorations of Masonic Geometry and Symbolry being a Dissertation on the Lost Knowledge of the Lodge*, (1905).
14 Val Brinkerhoff. *Day Star: Reading Sacred Architecture*. (2009) Digital Legend Press, New York
15 Alonzo L. Gaskill. "The Seal of Melchizedek?" (2010) *The Religious Educator* 11, (3) 95-121. Downloaded Feb 27, 2015 at http://rsc.byu.edu/pt-pt/archived/volume-11-number-3-2010/seal-melchizedek-0
16 Juan Eduardo Cirlot. *A Dictionary of Symbols*. (2002) Courier Dover p. 122.
17 Laleh Bakhtiar. *Sufi Expression of the Mystic Quest*. Avon (1976)
18 Schneider. *Op cite*.
19 Alan Rex Mitchell. *Melchizedek's Seal & Scroll* (2012) Greenjacket Books, Vernon, Utah. Available on amazon.com.

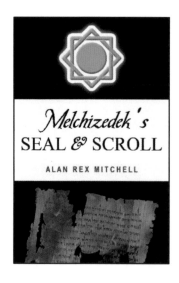

Made in the USA
Charleston, SC
17 July 2016